Lifeline

Carla

May God continue to speak volumes
of words to you and shower you with
His love. May your Kindness continue
to bless those you encounter. I pray
your purpose & destiny be fruitful
forever.

Pastor Shirley Jones

Lifeline

When God Speaks

Shirley J. Jones

Kingdom Living Publishing
Fort Washington, MD

Cover design by Tamika L. Hayden, TLH Designs, Chicago, IL (www.tlhdesigns.com)

Published by:

Kingdom Living Publishing
10907 Livingston Road
Fort Washington, MD 20744

Published in the United States of America.

ISBN 978-0-9799798-4-2

There is nothing that compares to when God speaks words of encouragement, revelation, and wisdom to you. My life has so changed from the first words He spoke to me, "I love you. You are special to me."

Dedication

In loving memory of my son, Rasheen Aaron Jones. You are still encouraging me to be about my Father's business. At your home-going service, twenty-one people gave their lives to the Lord. I pray that I continue to listen and avail myself to the Lord for others. Forever loving you, Rasheen.

Mom

⁗⁗

Rasheen Aaron Jones

Home-Going: June 3, 1997

⁗⁗

Acknowledgments

Father God, thank You for Your love towards me and for Your faithfulness. Wow! Life with and in You is so awesome. I look forward to the further unfolding of destiny and purpose. Hallelujah!

Jamal and Hasan, I am so proud to be your mom as I see you both walking and grabbing the words spoken over your life. Men not perfect but seeking the wisdom of God.

My daughters-in-law, Tai and Angel, thanks for loving my boys; and glad we three wear the same shoe size (smile).

My grandchildren, Nigel, Niylah, Madison, and Manuel, you represent life to me.

Pastor Irma McKnight, for always pushing and helping me move forward in words and deeds. You are one of the kindest and most know-how people I have ever known. Glad you are a part of my life forever. Once again you said, "Here's a book."

Rehoboth Family Life Center, thank you for your prayers and support. I thank God for a people willing to work and serve God. Church not as usual.

Table of Contents

Foreword One

It is the most incredible experience to be living within God's plan; especially when you do not realize it until almost twenty years later. I cannot remember a time when my mother did not speak a word into my life. She has always been a praying woman. I will have to admit that it was not until my mid twenties that I developed my own personal relationship with our Lord, Jesus Christ. Through the prayers and beliefs of my mother, I knew He existed. In all situations, good, bad, and the toughest of times, my mother's suggestion would be "Let's say a prayer." Whether I was miles away from our home in Philadelphia in another state or oversees in the Navy, she would say, "Let me pray for you over the phone." At thirty-nine years of age, I can tell you first hand, "Prayer works."

I would have never thought that through all those years God was training and equipping my mother to be a pastor. As I think back over the years, I can understand now why she made the choices she made and how she has been able to grow into the woman you know today. I heard it in sermons numerous times, "God has a plan for your life" and "Only God knows what the future holds." I feel so blessed that God allowed me to watch Him at work, while He held my mother's hand as He walked with her through lesson after lesson to bring forth Pastor Shirley Jones. Thank you Jesus!

For me—a person still growing in my relationship with Jesus—I find it very difficult sometimes to understand how the sermon I just heard relates to me and my needs. Therefore, I love a pastor who can take the Word of God and make it practical to what I am dealing with in my daily life. The *Lifeline* series does just that. It makes the Word of God useful.

Walking with God is like being dropped off in a foreign country with no map. In order to stay safe and move in the right direction, you need to feel His presence and know the sound of His voice. If you are not clear on what His directions are for your life you are going to find yourself confused and constantly in trouble. Since God is not a person that you can call, text, email, or just sit down and talk to in the natural, the Words provided in the Bible are your only true connection to Him. *Lifeline: When God Speaks* helps to make what you read in the Word clear; and it reminds you of what God has for you. You can consider *Lifeline: When God Speaks* your compass and the Bible your map. I use them both and have been amazed by the blessings I have experienced and how my life has been positively affected.

Jamal E. Jones

Foreword Two

I feel that the words from a mother are the words from our Father above. The power of God flows though the bond of a mother and child.

I have known Pastor Shirley Jones all my life, 30 years. And for those entire 30 years, the Lord has been in our life in some form or fashion. My mother's walk has been my walk as well. So I can truly say the Lord has His finger on her life and that the words you will read in *Lifeline: When God Speaks* are straight from our Lord Jesus Christ.

I recommend these pages on the bases of how the Lord has moved in my life. The guidance given from my mother, Pastor Shirley Jones, has been the stepping stones to my abundance.

Hasan Q. Jones

Introduction

The most fulfilling and awe-inspiring times of my life are when God speaks to me. Nothing else compares to those times. From the very beginning, when I learned to hear His voice—telling me that I would be okay and how special I was to Him and just calling me by name— it healed my broken pieces. His spoken Words of life have been forever beckoning me on a journey with Him.

Lifeline: When God Speaks was birthed out of times of Him speaking life to me that I may speak to others. I forever wait to hear from Him to know what to do in every situation in my life. He has been ever so faithful to me. I pray that these words of life will become your words of life. When God speaks, anything and everything do happen. I have found life in His Words and I pray you will, too.

Lifelines, the words that push and position us forward.

Part One

Do Not Move

Don't Die in the Wilderness

The Israelites were within an 11-day journey to the land that God promised them. They were told to go and possess the land, but they wanted to go and spy out the land first. God appeased them and instructed Moses to have one ruler from each of the twelve tribes go and spy out the land for forty days. Ten of the spies came back with a report that the land was a prosperous place, but that the men were greater than them and they would not survive. Joshua was in agreement with Caleb that they could possess the land: *And Caleb stilled the people before Moses, and said, Let us go up at once, and possess it: for we are well able to overcome it* (Numbers 13:30). However, the people accepted the evil report of the ten and rebelled against Moses and Aaron and wanted to go back to Egypt.

Moses convinced God not to destroy everyone because of their unbelief of the promise that the land was theirs. God pronounced judgment against the people that everyone twenty and older would wander in the wilderness for forty years and die off, one year for every day that they scouted out the land. Only those under twenty would enter the Promised Land. The ten spies with the evil report were smitten by a plague and died.

What has God promised you? Regardless of what it looks like—the obstacles and the naysayers—know that He is faithful and more than able to do anything but fail. Do not allow the enemy to prolong your journey into your Promised Land. You are so close to what you have been waiting for, eleven days or forty years. Believe, follow instructions, and receive!

Numbers 13:30

Relentless

"**Stop!!!** This is not the time to move or come up with your own plans of deliverance. The whole objective of the enemy is to cause you to move out of place so that when the answer, blessing, and deliverance come they will find you out of position to receive what you have long been waiting for. The time is shorter now than ever before. Hold fast and be **relentless** no matter what comes your way. It is a distraction to force you out of position. Don't move! Just press into Me even the more."

My soul, wait thou only upon God; for my expectation is from Him. He only is my rock and my salvation; He is my defense; I shall not be moved.

Psalm 62:5-6

Suddenly and Immediately

"My children, now is not the time to doubt, fear, get weary, make a decision, or be led astray to go to the city to satisfy any fleshly lust. Know this: The enemy is waiting and lurking around for the opportunity to get you off course and out of position for your suddenly and your immediately. Please, not now! Stay ever before Me and satiate yourself in My Word that you do not give wind to the pull of your flesh or not be able to advert the attack of the enemy on your blindside. What you miss, my Spirit in you will not miss. Allow the Holy Spirit to lead and guide you down the backstretch to your next place of destiny. Not now! Everything in you, around you, and about you must be brought into subjection to the leading of the Holy Spirit. Follow His lead only. Not now! Look for the light of day—the new thing that awaits you. Not now! I have you. For suddenly it shall appear. Selah."

Being confident of this very thing, that He who hath begun a good work in you will perform it unto the day of Jesus Christ.

Philippians 1:6

Strategies

"I am a strategic God who moves only once to bring about life changes. Most times You ask Me to intervene in your present situations and I am thinking and moving far ahead. Remember, I am eternity, so everything you will ever need or experience has already been done and appropriated. What you are asking will only quiet and satisfy your soul for now, but I am putting in place components that will change your life forever. Life changes, not moment changes. Let Me finish My orchestration of your life plans so that I can unveil My master plan and change your life and propel you forward. I am God and do all things greatly. Suddenly it shall appear; wherein you shall be glad. Strategies will unfold. Know My master plan is taking you forward to purpose and destiny. Life changes!"

The glory of this latter house shall be greater than of the former, saith the Lord of hosts: and in this place will I give peace, saith the Lord of hosts.

Haggai 2:9

Part Two

In His Hands

Shoot Thee as an Arrow

It is so awesome to know that the Lord has not only known us, but called us by name before time. He is perfecting us to be able to be weapons in His hand against the powers of darkness. A quiver is a container that holds the arrows and is usually worn on the back or side of a warrior. The quiver keeps the arrows secure and protected for the time of war. Just think, God is now hiding you by His side preparing you for use. And at the appointed time, He will launch you forward to do His purpose in the earth—restore mankind. So... do not become anxious, doubtful, or fearful. Know that your Daddy has you close to Him, covered by His presence. And know that every trial, tribulation, and challenge help sharpen you, the arrow, and make you ready to be sent forth. You are a weapon under construction. Let it happen.

Listen O isles unto me and harken ye people from far: The Lord hath called me from the womb; from the body of my mother hath he made mention of my name. And he hath made my mouth like a sharp sword; in the shadow of his hand hath he hidden me and made me a polished shaft; in his quiver hath he hidden me.

Isaiah 49:1-2

I Am the God of More than Enough

In Kenya recently, more than 100 people died and another 200 or more people were badly burned after someone in the crowd lit a cigarette, while they were siphoning fuel out of an overturned tanker. An impoverished people were trying to get some relief, even only for a day. Desperate people do desperate acts and wisdom is tossed to the wind. They did not know the God who is more than enough.

After losing their jobs, a husband and wife in California discussed their situation and decided their only solution was to end their lives. The husband killed his wife and their children. Then after reporting what he had done, he killed himself. Hopeless people do desperate things and wisdom is tossed to the wind.

In the midst of economic unrest, do not allow your focus to be on what is wrong; but on the truth that we serve the God of more than enough. I rebuke the spirit of hopelessness that has been released on the earth. We must keep our focus on "Abba" so that we will be kept in perfect peace. The economy will recover; but as we pray and wait, we must stand trusting God for everything we need. I declare no lack, just victory, as we agree, "He is the God of more than enough."

*The earth is the Lord's and the fulness thereof;
the world and they that dwell therein.*

Psalm 24:1

*For the Lord God will help me; therefore shall
I not be confounded: therefore have I set my
face like a flint, and I know that I shall not be
ashamed.*

Isaiah 50:7

He Will Always Be with Us

"I know and understand you better than anyone else, including you. I know your beginning and your end. I know your thoughts afar off; and for every situation and circumstance with which you are confronted, provisions have already been appropriated through eternity. I endured the cross, the time of separation from the Father, which was the hardest part of the crucifixion, that you need not experience the separation ever. Everything that I endured need never be repeated, because I am the ultimate sacrifice. I am with you and in you forever more. Amen."

Seeing then that we have a great high priest, that is passed into the heavens, Jesus the Son of God, let us hold fast our profession. For we have not an high priest which cannot be touched with the feeling of our infirmities; but was in all points tempted like as we are, yet without sin. Let us therefore come boldly unto the throne of grace, that we may obtain mercy, and find grace to help in time of need.

Hebrews 4:14-16

The Process

Most of us dislike the process of becoming; we just want to become. I attribute this to the fact that we live in a society where everything is so fast paced and there are only a few things for which we have to wait. Becoming a vessel unto righteousness in the Kingdom of God involves a progression of events, people, and places. The process of becoming exposes us to the attributes of God (faithfulness, mind keeper, peace giver, provider, etc.) and wisdom that is forever ours and that we will need later on our journey. So let your process of becoming happen according to the will of God for your life.

I speak right now to your emotions and say, "Be still." I pray that your emotions do not over take you and become the ruling factor in your life. May your spirit keep you and guide you through your process of becoming all that God has purposed you to be. Joseph's process took him from the pit to the palace. Where will your process take you?

The best awaits you!

To everything there is a season and a time to every purpose under the heaven... He hath made every thing beautiful in His time...
                                    Ecclesiastes 3:1a, 11a

When?

We all from one time or another, and even now, have asked God, "When?" In the book of 1 Samuel, Chapter 1, we find Hannah who is barren married to Elkanah. He is also married to Peninah, who has given him ten sons and daughters. According to the Mishnah (Jewish oral law), a man married to a woman who could not have any children after ten years could and was instructed to take on another wife so that the word "be fruitful and multiply" could be fulfilled. At least twenty years had passed and Hannah was still barren. The Scriptures tell us that Peninah was Hannah's adversary, because Elkanah loved Hannah more. Peninah had the babies, but Hannah had his heart.

I know that during times of ridicule from Peninah, from other folks, and from Hannah just feeling inadequate, she asked God "When?" Finally on one of their yearly trips to sacrifice to the Lord, Hannah reached the point of being sick and tired of being sick and tired (Have you ever been there?) and rose up from the table and got before the Lord in prayer. This time she vowed that if God would just bless her with a male child, she would give him to the Lord to serve Him forever. The vow and prayer were blessed by Eli the priest and received by God. Thus she conceived and Samuel was born.

It was not until she got in agreement with the plan of God that He moved. She had been asking for a baby for twenty years or more; but God had a plan. In those days there was no king in Israel. Everyone did what was right in his own eyes. Thus Samuel. Hannah wanted a baby, but God was calling forth a prophet, a judge, and a king maker to Israel.

What are you called to birth out into the earth? I know that it is bigger than you. Trust Him; satiate yourself in the Word; stay prayerful; choose your company wisely; and keep oil in your lamps!

The "when" will produce the greater in you!

The Lord is not slack concerning His promise, as some men count slackness; but is longsuffering to usward.

2 Peter 3:9a

Who and Whose Are You

In this next part of life, we all must know who and whose we are. Remember the Vanderbilts? They are one of the most famous families in the country. There are just certain things that the Vanderbilts just would not be caught doing, wearing, and speaking; or places they would not be caught staying. There is a standard of living that has been passed down through the generations that all display the mark of the Vanderbilts. When the name is mentioned, people automatically expect and express a certain attitude and behavior. They knew certain things and would not settle for anything less.

We have been born again into a royal family with an everlasting inheritance; and a place has been carved out for us upon the earth. We must know it and walk in it. David was more than a shepherd boy, he was a king. Esther was more than a queen; she was a deliverer. Jesus was more than a prophet; He is a Savior. Let the more of you be birthed out as you really realize who and whose you are.

What is man, that thou are mindful of him? and the son of man, that thou visitest him? For thou hast made him a little lower than the angles and hast crowned him with glory and honour. Thou madest him to have dominion over the works of thy hands: thou hast put all things under his feet.

Psalm 8:4-6

Reference: http://en.wikipedia.org/wiki/Vanderbilt_family

Part Three

Getting to the Other Side

Step into the Deep

Several months ago I had a dream of standing at the bank of a river. There were people traveling the different roads to the river like me. We all crossed the river each day to get to the other side where we worked. This particular day the river was high. I stood and watched the first person step in and the water came to mid-chest. The second person stepped in and went a little further and the water covered their head. I stood there wondering how I was going to get to work, because I could not swim. As I stood, there two lady friends walked up and asked me if I was going to work. I responded that the river was too high and I could not swim. They assured me not to worry because they would hold me on each side and get me across. When I awoke, the Lord spoke to me to not be afraid to step into the deep and that He had already positioned those to help me get to the other side… destiny.

So…, what has God spoken to you through dreams and visions with interpretation to take you further on your road of destiny? It is not enough to have dreams and visions. What do we do with them? Let us take the necessary steps to get to the other side for what awaits us. Push away from the shore-line of comfort and familiarity.

See you there!!!!!!

Pour Out Your Best Offering—You

"My children, I love you with an everlasting love; and I have always loved you. I know the plans I have for your life and you shall be glad. You are called to do great exploits upon the earth in My name. Do not shy away from Me. I desire all of you. Haven't I proven myself faithful time and time again? Have I not loved you through your broken places? Then you should know you can trust Me with you—all of you! Give Me access to everything you are about and who you are. No bars. Total surrender to Me yields total freedom in Me. What do I need to do to get the rest of you? The hour is late and there is much work to be done upon the earth. None of you and all of Me. Yield now to My hand and My love. Haven't I proven myself?"

And behold, a woman in the city, which was a sinner, when she knew that Jesus sat at meat in the Pharisee's house, brought an alabaster box of ointment. And she stood at his feet behind him weeping, and began to wash his feet with tears, and did wipe them with the hairs of her head, and kissed his feet, and anointed them with the ointment.

Luke 7:37-38

Expecting? Are You Really?

If you were expecting to move, you would begin to throw some old stuff out (at least you should), pack boxes, and envision how you are going to set the new place up. Expecting to move in the Spirit is really no different. Take stock of where you are and allow the Holy Spirit to search you and instruct you on the things that just cannot go into the next part of your life. Be determined not to continue to carry from place to place baggage of unforgiveness, procrastination, negativity, fear, some folks, and insecurity. There is a new place set up for you. Get to work and do not be your own stumbling block. Expecting?

Even so faith, if it hath not works, is dead, being alone. Yea, a man may say, Thou hast faith, and I have works: shew me thy faith without thy works, and I will shew thee my faith by my works.

James 2: 17-18

Do Not Shrink Back Now

"New opportunities, open doors, extended spheres of influence. Do not shrink back because you feel you cannot do it. Let my Word "I can do all things through Christ who strengthens me" forever resonate within you. New beginnings are just that—new. Embrace the things that I am bringing before you. Everything that you will need, you can find in Me. I am also sending people to walk beside you who are versed in areas that you have not been stretched in yet. My work in the earth will not be hindered, but shall forge forth in this season. Your latter should be greater than your former. Greater works shall you do. Do not shrink back. Rise up and be counted among those being used during harvest time. Come forth now and do My bidding in the earth. The harvest is plentiful but the laborers are few. Will you say yes today?"

Brethren, I count not myself to have apprehended: but this one thing I do, forgetting those things which are behind, and reaching forth unto those things which are before. I press toward the mark for the prize of the high calling of God in Christ Jesus.

Philippians 3: 13-14

Through

God would never take you to it or allow it to show up in front of you and not bring you through it. We serve an awesome God, who is omnipotent (infinite in power; having very great or unlimited authority or power). The Bible tells us that the Word was *"written for our learning, that we through patience and comfort of the Scriptures might have hope"* (Romans 15:4). Remember, when the Israelites got to the Red Sea, Moses stretched out his rod and the waters parted and the people went over on dry land. And when the Egyptians tried to come after them, the waters returned in place; and the riders and the horses were destroyed. God not only brought the Israelites to the Red Sea, but He took them through it. Moses told the people that the Egyptians whom they had seen on that day they would see them again no more forever.

God remains the same today as yesterday and forever more. So do not fret, but stand still and wait on your instructions to go through the obstacles that stand before you. They may seem insurmountable— maybe for you, but not for Almighty God. He will take you through it. With Him, there is no respect of persons. If He did it for them at the Red Sea, and again at the Jordan River, He will do it for you. Let Him take you through it!

For with God nothing shall be impossible.
Luke 1:37

Part Four

New Day

Morning

Morning... regardless of how bad yesterday was, no matter the wrong choices we made, this morning is new. I love mornings because of the opportunity to do differently, see differently, and experience something that I have never experienced. God's tender mercies are new each and every morning. So... look for the new mercies and benefits that He loads us with daily. Do not miss it by complaining about what is not or blaming yourself, but be excited and look for what is new. **Good morning!!!!**

It is of the Lord mercies that we are not consumed, because His compassions fail not. They are new every morning; great is thy faithfulness.

Lamentation 3:22-23

Blessed be the Lord who daily loadeth us with benefits even the God of our salvation.

Psalm 69:19

Live

Life! Is there a silent thought brewing inside of you that says, "There has to be more to life than what I am living?" There is!!! I believe that life is a series of events geared toward purpose and enjoyment of the things that are attached to how we have been wired. For example, I know my purpose is to preach, teach the gospel, and make disciples. I love fresh cut flowers and dinner on outside spaces. One weekend I cut fresh flowers from my yard and had dinner on my deck—two things that are me. In order to not allow discontentment, disappointment, and complacency to set in, learn your purpose and how you are wired and do you!! Wirings are those simple unique things that make up who we are. Life is so much more than merely existing. He has come to give us life and life more abundantly. Live!!!!!!!!

The thief cometh not but to steal, and to kill, and to destroy; I am come that they might have life and that they might have it more abundantly.

John 10:10

Forgiven

"I love you with an everlasting love. My love for you has never been based on your rights and wrongs, but because I am love. Haven't I already shown you how special you are to Me by the "Cross." I gave My best for the best of Me—you. You are forgiven My child, so let us get back on track toward your path of destiny and purpose. Now that I have forgiven you, you forgive you. Destiny and purpose await you round the bend. I am with you and in you always. Let's go!"

It is of the Lord's mercies that we are not consumed, because His compassions fail not. They are new every morning; great is thy faithfulness.

Lamentations 3:22

Part Five

My Daughters

Come

"My daughters, I am calling you closer to Me so that you may experience My glory and have it become your resting and dwelling place. Some of you are carrying burdens that are much too heavy for you that should be given over to Me. What appears to be impossible for you is nothing for Me. The burdens are weighing you down and hindering you from moving forward on your road of destiny and purpose. There is so much more that I have for you. Abandon your worries, fears, doubts, and apprehensions to Me this day and allow Me to move you forward. Let Me become your place of peace and rest. I do have so much more waiting for you. Come! Come now. The hour is late. Come now, daughters!"

Come unto Me, all ye that labour and are heavy laden, and I will give you rest. Take My yoke upon you, and learn of Me; for I am meek and lowly in heart: and ye shall find rest unto your souls. For My yoke is easy and My burden is light.

Matthew 11:28-30

Come Now

"Tell them to come and commune with Me. I await the presence of My children. The sacrifice has been made and the curtain rent, so come and have audience with Me. There is so much I desire to share out of the mystery of My Word, that it no longer is a mystery, but truth that your life may be governed to your destiny. Come! I await the next level of intimacy from glory to glory. Come, my beloved daughters. The table has been set and the finest has been laid out just for you. Come!!!!"

There remaineth therefore a rest to the people of God.

Hebrews 4:9

Behold, I stand at the door and knock. If anyone hears My voice and opens the door, I will come in to him and dine with him, and he with Me.

Revelation 3:20

Fragmented Souls Becoming Whole

"Daughters, not just friends, but daughters. I call you today to come in closer to Me. Come and sit in My presence as a way of life and not because you are in want. I desire all of you so that My presence can satiate every area of your life. Yes, you have asked and received salvation, but there is so much more of Me that I desire to give to you. Come now; the hour is late and I so desire the best for you and in you. The fragmented parts of your soul need to be healed that you may be made whole. Only sitting before Me will allow this to happen. The best of you is still to come, be seen, and experienced by you. Then I can truly thrust you out into a lost world as my ambassador to redeem those with fragmented souls.

Come now; the hour is late, daughters!"

And the very God of peace sanctify you wholly, and I pray God your whole spirit and soul and body be preserved blameless unto the coming of our Lord Jesus Christ.

1 Thessalonians 5:23

Part Six

Gird Up

Distractions

Everyone and everything that God loves, the enemy hates. Satan is always looking for means to have you discredit God and prevent or delay purpose in your life. He uses distractions such as family members, finances, work, health issues, wanting to belong, and our fears and insecurities to get our focus off what God has called for us.

Do not be deceived. If the serpent was brazen (old folk's term) enough to work his craftiness in the garden, he is not afraid to come after you. He is not an imaginary character walking around with a pitchfork, long tail, horns, and a red suit. He is a spirit, but not the Spirit. He needs a body to operate in that looks just like you. He will use whoever is not submitted to Christ.

We must satiate ourselves in the Word of God and commit to God everyone and everything around us and attached to us. Distractions will come, but God is so much greater than them all. Guessing is over. You must know who is greater—God!

The thief cometh not but to steal, and to kill, and to destroy; I am come that they might have life and that they might have it more abundantly.

John 10:10

Guarding Your Powerhouse: The Holy Spirit

"I am the door; by me if any man enters in, he shall be saved, and shall go in and out, and find pasture. The thief cometh not, but for to steal, and to kill, and to destroy; I am come that they might have life, and that they might have it more abundantly. I am the good shepherd; the good shepherd giveth his life for the sheep."

John 10:9-11

The Greater One lives within every believer and is operating when given permission. This year let us purpose to let the Holy Spirit have rule in all that we are and do:

1. Abide and dwell in the safety of the Almighty God (John 15:4, Psalm 91:1-2)

2. Obtain wisdom - get your instructions from within (Proverbs 8:32-36). Abba must be your everything (Psalm 18:2)

3. Pray (1 Thessalonians 5:17)

4. Worship - (John: 23-24)

62

5. Let the Holy Spirit develop your moral character (Romans 8:1-17, Galatians 5:16-26, Proverbs 14:12)

6. Watch your associations (Galatians 5:9, Amos 3:3, 1 John 4:1, Ephesians 4:14)

7. Guard your tongue (Proverbs 15:4, Psalm 34:13, Proverbs 18:21)

8. Watch you—allow the Holy Spirit to reveal the weak and fragile areas of your life (Psalm 51)

9. Do not let pride find a resting place—you are not all that! (Isaiah 42:8a, Proverbs 16:18)

Now unto him that is able to keep you from falling, and to present you faultless before the presence of His glory with exceeding joy, to the only wise God our Saviour, be glory and majesty, dominion and power, both now and ever. Amen.

Jude 24-25

The Builder Is God

As you are moving on your path of God's expected end for your life, let Him lead and direct you. There are new places and opportunities that you have never experienced. Stay on post and pay attention as not to get caught on your blind side. Keep your armor shined, with all the parts operating properly. Keep the wick trimmed and oil in your lamps. Trust God, but tie up your camel (old Arab Proverb). Even in the new places, traps are still set. God, the Master Builder, knows where everything is and who everybody really is. Lines have been drawn to keep you on track. The Holy Spirit will quicken you when you step out of the path of your expected end. Stay sensitive to the move of the Holy Spirit and just let God do this!

Except the Lord build the house, they labour in vain that build it: except the Lord keep the city, the watchman waketh but in vain. It is vain for you to rise up early; to set up late to eat the bread of sorrows: for so He giveth His beloved sleep.

Psalm 127:1-2

Urgency of Prayer—SOS

"There are things, circumstances, and even people that are infiltrating our personal life, our family, our jobs, our neighborhoods, and the world in which we live. You do not have to take less or accept ungodliness or unrighteousness. You need not become overwhelmed, anxious, or hopeless; but come before Me in prayer to remain focused and to become an instrument in My hand so that the tide of time will change forever. I speak to your emotions today and command them to "be still." Use the weapon of prayer that will cause things to radically change and get in order. Would I, your Father God, leave you defenseless? What kind of Father would I be?

Your latter shall be greater. Now you command the rest to change around you including the world. PRAY. There is urgency now!"

The effectual fervent prayer of a righteous man availeth much. 2010 there are no gray areas. Either God or the enemy; yielded harvest of righteousness or unrighteousness.

James 5:1b

Part 7

He Wants to Speak to You

Divine Revelation

"My dear children, there is so much that I desire to share with you—especially the upcoming events on the earth. I want you to be prepared to avoid the upheavals and to experience My glory. I am about to move mightily upon the earth; and I am calling My sons and daughters from the four corners of the earth to come and commune with Me. Once again, allow Me to position you strategically so that you will be a part of My plan. Listen, stay focused, and be not distracted, as I will continually provide your every need. In this season, I am calling you to be a beacon light to a lost world.

Circumstances—unexplainable circumstances—will force many to seek Me out, since nothing else will suffice. Embrace them and allow My glory to be revealed through you. This is new and has never graced the earth before. Do not allow anyone to tell you differently. I am doing a new thing and declare that you be a part of this movement. Greater anointing. Get under the flow of it to stay renewed and ready. A new thing and I do declare it before it springs forth."

Behold, the former things are come to pass, and new things do I declare: before they spring forth I tell you of them.

Isaiah 42:9

A Clarion Call

It is time for God to become our priority. Look around and see all the things that are happening upon the earth. The lion is loosed out of the thicket looking for whom he can devour. Therefore, your dwelling place must be in Christ. You may not get a chance to get back to the fortified city. Come and make your dwelling place sure. No time to wonder or not know where you live. Gather your family and stay put!!!!!!

He that dwelleth in the secret place of the most High shall abide under the shadow of the Almighty. I will say of the Lord, He is my refuge and my fortress: my God; in Him will I trust.

Psalm 91:1-2

Take Me Out of the Box

How many times do we pray and say we are trusting God, but we have readymade timelines and even come up with how God is going to move?

I hear the Lord say this morning, "Take me out of the box. My Word declares in Isaiah 55:8-9, *"For my thoughts are not your thoughts, neither are your ways my ways saith the Lord. For as the heavens are higher than the earth, so are My ways higher than your ways, and My thoughts than your thoughts."* Signs and wonders will follow those who believe.

Stop applying your ordinary ways to the magnificence of Me. I am not doing it your way, but Mine, so that My glory may be revealed through the earth. Take Me out of the box and let Me show you great and mighty things. The heavens declare My glory. What about you?"

Shut the Door

I challenge you for the next seven days to spend time with the Lord. Shut the door to your mind, eyes, ears and mouth. Let everything that you do be done to the glory of God. After Noah, his family, and the animals went into the ark as instructed, God shut them in. After the rain ceased and the waters receded off the earth, Noah and all that was in the ark became the elements for new life. Shut the door and then step into the new life that will await you.

And they that went in, went in male and female of all flesh, as God had commanded him: and the LORD shut him in.

Genesis 7:16

And ye shall not go out of the door of the tabernacle of the congregation in seven days, until the days of your consecration be at an end: for seven days shall he consecrate you.

Leviticus 8:33

We Are the Church

What causes a church to start out on fire and then slowly the anointing and presence of God are no longer there? The church service is still going on, the choir is singing, and the preacher is preaching, but the lives of the people remain the same. The issue is with us, because we are the church.

Church must always be about God for the healing and deliverance of the people. It should never be about the people for the people, because then God is cancelled out of the equation. Then what is the point? Let us honestly examine ourselves and see if our hearts are bent to loving God and His people or just the notion of church—works and fulfilling our religious obligations and traditions.

Let us return, or for some, even start making our love relationship with God the most important part of our life. Then we can be the church and not just have church.

Thou shalt love the Lord thy God with all thy heart, and with all thy soul, and with all thy strength and with all thy mind; and thy neighbor as thyself.

Luke 10:27

Hanker Down

Hanker down is not a term that I use in my everyday conversation. It means to settle in at a location for an extended period of time; to maintain a position and resist yielding to some pressure as of public opinion; to take shelter; to assume a defensive position to resist difficulties; hide out; to keep out of sight as for protection and safety; hold firm, stand fast—refuse to abandon one's opinion or belief.

We must find our resting place in our Lord. Get a song, get a word, stay on your face, and hanker down. Do not be moved by the storms of life or the things that come to challenge you. Remember, when the disciples and Jesus were on the ship and the storm arose and the ship became full of water? They began to panic, but he slept. They woke Him up and He spoke to the winds and rains, "peace be still;" and the sea became calm again. He challenged them letting them know that because He was on the ship everything would be all right. He is with you and will never forsake you. Hanker down and be ready to move at a moment's notice to your next place of destiny and purpose. Do not be moved. The Captain of your ship is on board. Hanker down!

You are my resting place, oh Lord
I trust you, I love you, I need you forever more
You are my resting place, oh Lord
I trust you, I love you, I need you forever more
You are my rest, you are my rest, you are my rest-
ing place.*

*There remaineth therefore a rest to the people
of God. For he that is entered into his rest, he
also hath ceased from his own works, as God
did from His. Let us labour therefore to enter
into the rest, lest any man fall after the same
example of unbelief.*

Hebrew 4:9-11

*Prophetic song by Shirley J. Jones, Copyright 2010

Thirty Days

The number three means to conform (obey; copy; imitate and likeness). On the third day of creation, God continued to speak and then creation conformed to what was being spoken: And God said, *Let the waters under the heavens be gathered together unto one place, and let the dry land appear; and it was so* (Genesis 1:9). The number thirty means acceptably conformed. Levites had to be thirty years old before they could become a priest or serve in the tabernacle. And David was thirty when he began to reign. The use of the number thirty is best illustrated with Jesus. He did not begin His ministry until age thirty. Yet, the Gospel of John tells us that if all of the things He did were written down one by one, the world could not contain all of the books that would be written (John 21:25).

God spoke to me and said "I am not only speaking to the women at the Bible Study [Arise Ministries], but to whoever has an ear to hear and will obey. Come before Me for thirty days, where nothing matters to you as much as I do. Yes, you are going to be distracted and challenged, but know that this time will cause some shackles and chains to be broken. So be determined to stay close to My bosom until you become as "acceptably conformed" as was My dearly loved Son, in whom I am well pleased. I so desire My sentiments to be the same for you."

Thirty days!!!

For whom He did foreknow, He also did predestinate to be conformed to the image of His Son.

Romans 8:29a

It Is Still About Righteousness

From the very beginning in Genesis 1:26, God said, *"Let us make man in our image, after our likeness and let them have dominion over the fish of the sea, and over the fowl of the air, and over the cattle and over the earth and over every creeping thing upon the earth."* Well, the script has not changed and their (God, Jesus, and the Holy Spirit) design upon us is still righteousness. Do not lose sight; not now. Remember, Jesus is looking to present to Himself a glorious church, not having a spot, or wrinkle, or any such thing; but that it should be holy and without blemish (Ephesians 5:27). We are the church. Are there spots in your love feast toward the Lord or are you more concerned about provisions and not the giver of provisions?

Righteous living can cause things to happen in our life and others. Abraham was able to covenant with God for the life of Lot and his family based on having ten righteous in Sodom and Gomorrah. King Hezekiah reminded God of his righteous living, after being told by the prophet Isaiah that he was going to die. God healed him, added 15 years to his life, and gave him victory over the enemy.

Until our last day upon this earth, let us continue to pray Psalm 139: 23-24: *Search me, O God, and know my heart: try me and know my thoughts: and see if there be any wicked way in me and lead me in the way everlasting.* Amen!

Part 8

Forgive

FATHER GOD

Some of us have had fathers who in our thought patterns were not real fathers. I have learned that people can only do what they know to do and have been exposed to themselves. If we look closely at their own lives, we see lacks and unrest caused by others. Let us purpose in our hearts to forgive as we have been forgiven so we can embrace the path of destiny that Father God has for us.

The best of fathers cannot even compare to Father God. Why?

+   He knew us before we were formed in our mother's womb (Jeremiah 1:5a);

+   He gave the best for us, the best of Him - His Son Jesus Christ (John 3:16);

+   He never disappoints us. His promises are yea and amen (2 Corinthians 1:20);

+   He supplies all our need (Philippians 4:19);

+   He gives His angels charge over us to keep us in all our ways (Psalm 91:11);

+   He has destiny and purpose mapped out for us (Jeremiah 29:11);

+ He chastises us because He loves us (Proverbs 3:11-12); and

+ He has given us the gift of salvation, made us heirs to everything He has and is, and has given us the promise of eternal life (Romans 8:14-18).

Let us forgive and embrace Father God!

The Spirit of Unity

Whatever God blesses the enemy attempts to change it so the blessings will no longer be attached to it. Psalm 133 declares that where unity is "there the Lord commanded the blessing, even life forever more." Now do you see why the enemy has attacked your marriage and relationships with family members, a brethren at your church, a co-worker, a neighbor, or a friend? The enemy is trying to have your blessings nullified because of contention, strife, and quarreling.

Endeavor to keep the unity. Love and forgive as you have been from the Lord. There is power in numbers and blessings commanded toward you forever more when unity is present. Let us all come together and wreck havoc with the enemy and stay in position of our blessings. I need you and you need me. We are one and the same. Unity!

Behold, how good and how pleasant it is for brethren to dwell together in unity! It is like the precious ointment upon the head, that ran down upon the beard, even Aaron's beard: that went down to the skirts of his garments: As the dew of Hermon, and as the dew that descended upon the mountains of Zion: for there the Lord commanded the blessings, even life for evermore.

Psalm 133

Part 9

Celebrate

Sound of the Abundance of Rain

"There are elements of your life that shall manifest that will truly supersede all your thoughts and know-how. They belong totally to Me and shall be presented by Me. Jehovah is My name; and I am capable of all things that are beyond the natural realm and that come from the Spirit realm. Allow Me this day to further elevate your thinking and open your spiritual sight that you may see just a hint of all that is forthcoming. Your natural man will not be able to receive or keep up as things unfold. But your spirit already knows and is in cahoots with Me. Listen. You will hear it before you see it. Your rejoicing now will cause the plan to come in focus and manifest on the earth. Listen for the sound of blessing!"

For there is a sound of abundance of rain.
1 Kings 18: 41b

Fear not, little flock; for it is your Father's good pleasure to give you the Kingdom.
Luke 12:32

The Days After

One day of the year we celebrate Resurrection Sunday with church family, immediate family, and friends. The crucifixion, death, resurrection, and ascension of Jesus Christ have enabled believers to walk in forgiveness, authority, power, destiny, and purpose. Our Lord did all this for you and me. One day of celebration is not nearly enough. Let us celebrate every day with praise and thanksgiving. Let us be ready to point the lost to the One who was resurrected for all. Celebrate always!

And He is the propitiation for our sins: and not for ours only, but also for the sins of the whole world.

1 John 2:2

The Fickleness of Man

We want what we want, how we want it to be, when we want it to be; and it must be about us. When this does not happen, we can become angry and bitter, disappointed and depressed, withdrawn, and hopeless. We even declare murder, "Crucify Him!"

During Jesus' triumphal entry into Jerusalem, the people declared "Hosanna to the Son of David; Blessed is He that cometh in the name of the Lord; Hosanna in the highest." However, five days later, the cry from some of the same people was, "Crucify Him." They wanted Him to destroy the Roman rule, but Jesus came that all may be saved and have eternal life. They wanted what they wanted, but all things do work together. He died but rose with all power, anyhow.

Not just during Holy Week (time between Palm Sunday and the Resurrection), but every day of the week, let your "Hosanna in the highest" be heard and seen in everything you say and do. Do not crucify Him again with acts of disobedience when your ways do not work out. Show forth the grace of God that someone else may be saved. Hosanna!

A double minded man is unstable in all his ways.

James 1:5

Birthrights

When we give our life over to the Lord, there are provisions (birthrights) to which we become entitled. A few of them are:

+ He promises never to leave nor forsake us – Hebrews 13: 5b-6

+ Heirs of God and joint heirs with Jesus Christ – Romans 8:14-18

+ His promises are yea and amen – 2 Corinthians 1:20

+ Access to healing for us and others – Isaiah 53:5

+ Forgiveness of sin – Ephesians 1:7

+ Rest – Matthew 11:28-30

+ The faithfulness of God – Lamentations 3: 22-23

+ Indwelling of the Holy Spirit – John 16:7

+ Wisdom – James 1:5

+ Taken out of darkness – 1 Peter 2:9-10

+ New – 2 Corinthians 5:17

+ An expected end – Jeremiah 29:11

In the Book of Genesis, Chapter 25, Esau, the grandson of Abraham, sold his birthright to his brother, Jacob, for a bowl of stew. It is written that Esau despised his birthright. In other words, he had no reverence for his birthright. Do not become complacent in your relationship with God and all that He has provided for you. We nurture and protect things that are dear to us. Nurture and protect the birthrights given to you by God with this great salvation. Let there be no price tag on them that the enemy may seduce them from you. They are your birthrights keep them dear and near!

God Is Able

Has God ever failed you? Not have you always gotten what you wanted. But again, has He ever failed you? I have never had a situation or dilemma that God has not brought me through to the other side.

We serve an awesome and able God. He is able to do *exceeding, abundantly above all that we ask or think according to the power that works in us* (Ephesians 3:20). His credentials are sure. *In the beginning, God created the heaven and earth, when everything was without form and void: and darkness was upon the face of the deep* (Genesis 1:1-2). He just spoke and everything came into existence. Trust Him to speak and create in your situations.

Here in the Washington, DC, area this past winter (February 2010), we got a record breaking amount of snow of almost thirty inches. The area was shut down for a week or more. No matter what or how we felt, we had no control of how much snow we would get and when it would stop. Ironically, man has become capable of sending a man to the moon, producing artificial limbs, and discovering a number of cures and inventions. But every now and then God speaks by showing us who is in control and all that He is capable of doing: *Hast thou entered into the treasures of the snow? Or hast thou seen the*

94

treasures of the hail? Job 37:6a: for He saith to the snow, be thou on the earth (Job 38:22).

No matter where you may find yourself today, your situation is not greater than God or out of His reach. Trust and believe that is He is able. Hasn't he already proven Himself? Remind yourself of all the situations He has brought you through. He is the same yesterday, today, and forevermore. And if you have never trusted Him before, do it now and experience His greatness and love. God is able!

Part Ten

Prophetic Worship

Prophetic Worship

On the following pages are some of the prophetic worship songs the Lord has given me during my personal times of worship. Prophetic worship songs are birthed out of time spent before the Lord and in expressing one's gratitude. It has nothing to do with one's ability to sing, hit the high and low notes, or find the right key or pitch to sing in. I am an example of one who cannot tell an A sharp from a B flat; nor can I scale up and down. But I love God; and out of my personal time of prayer and worship, songs have been birthed. There is no certain setting in which this happens; it just happens. Actually, most times it is when I am driving in my car and just being so thankful that my words become songs. It is like the Holy Spirit within me partners with me during these times and we just magnify the Lord together.

At first and for some time, I would not dare sing anywhere but in my car, the shower, and at home. I then began to share the words and sing a little to those close to me because of being in awe and blessed by what I was given. Now I sing most of the songs with some of my messages, in the hospital interceding for someone sick, or for someone needing to just rest in the Lord.

So if someone like me with no music talent or know-how can worship, so can you. Open your mouth and proclaim your thanksgiving to the Lord and listen. Sing, sing, and sing unto the Lord a song that no one else has sung!

An Offering

I bring my life as an offering to you

I bring my life as an offering to you dear Lord

It's yours, it's yours, it's yours, it's yours

I bring my life as an offering to you

His Love

There is no greater love

Than Jesus Christ, the Lord our Lord

There is no greater love

He loved me then, He loves me now, He'll love me to
the end of time

There is no greater love

Than Jesus Christ, the Lord our Lord

There is no greater love

I Just Believe God

I just believe God

I believe, I believe God

I just believe God

I believe, I believe God

I just believe God

Note: Make this personal. Whatever you are believing God for say it; (e.g., I just believe God for healing, peace....)

Conclusion of the Matter

Father God wants to speak to His children and share the mysteries and the working mechanics of the Kingdom. So I pray now that your spiritual ears be open to the voice of your Lord and when He speaks, you shall hear and obey. Blessings in hearing words that will become your Lifeline!

Pastor Shirley J. Jones

Pastor Shirley J. Jones was born and raised in Philadelphia, PA. The Lord blessed her to be the very proud mother of three sons and the grandmother of four, two boys and two girls. She studied Liberal Arts at Temple University and attended Mount Airy Church of God in Christ Bible School in Philadelphia. She became very affluent in the insurance business, where she was employed in private sector for about 18 years. She currently works as a Quality Control Analyst for the federal government.

About 1984 life began to take a swirl downward, which caused Pastor Shirley to seek help and satisfaction that was not earthly but divine. That was the start of a divine journey that she has been on ever since. It has taken her from Philadelphia to Virginia to Maryland. Each stop has produced gains and losses, but above it all, she has received a further revelation of who her God is to her and her to Him. Her journey led to her being ordained a minister of the gospel in the office of the pastorate in June 1996.

She is the Senior Pastor of Rehoboth Family Life Center (RFLC), a ministry dedicated to the healing of families to heal the nations. She is the Director of Arise Ministries, a ministry geared toward women becoming healed and walking in their divine purpose. Called not only to speak the word, but also to write the word, in 1997 she authored her first book, "*Intimacy with God.*"

Pastor Shirley has declared that she should be about her Father's business and acknowledges that her life is to be an available vessel to be used to set the captives free. Her desire is to spend her remaining years furthering the Kingdom of God. She feels honored and so blessed that God would choose her to deliver His Word and to love His people. She gives Him all the glory. There is no other place that she would rather be than in the hands of her loving Father.

To inquire about speaking or ministry engagements, or teaching material, please contact:

Rehoboth Family Life Center
P.O.Box 154
Accokeek, MD 20607
pastorshirley@rehobothflc.org

For more information about this book, please contact:

Kingdom Living Publishing
10907 Livingston Road
Fort Washington, MD 20744
publish@kingdomlivingbooks.com
(301) 292-9010 / (877) 292-7733